Original title:

Life's Not About the Destination—It's About the Snacks

Copyright © 2025 Creative Arts Management OÜ
All rights reserved.

Author: Derek Caldwell
ISBN HARDBACK: 978-1-80566-059-0
ISBN PAPERBACK: 978-1-80566-354-6

The Snacks We Share

In a bowl, the popcorn pops,
While laughter fills the air.
Chips and dips will never stop,
It's fun beyond compare.

Salsa dances on our tongues,
Wings are flying high above.
Every bite a song that's sung,
A feast we dearly love.

Gatherings from the Journey

Travel snacks in every lane,
Choco bars and gummy bears.
Each pit stop's a sweet refrain,
With laughter in our affairs.

Tales unfold like rolling dough,
As pretzels twist around our fate.
Together on this snacky show,
We munch and celebrate.

Moments Cooked with Care

Oven warms with cheesy bliss,
Cookies rise like our delight.
Each detail a remembered kiss,
Baked together every night.

Pasta parties, bowls so full,
Spaghetti fests bring smiles galore.
Spoons are twirling, laughter's pull,
These moments we adore.

Cravings of the Curious

What's that crunch inside the bag?
Mystery nachos call my name.
Food adventures that we snag,
Each snack is fair game.

Taste of wonder, twist and turn,
Breadsticks beckon from the shelf.
In seeking snacks, we get to learn,
It's fun to feed ourselves!

The Snack That Stole Time

In a world of hustle, snack it slow,
Chips in hand, let the worries go.
Salsa dripping, laughter flows,
Conversations bloom, like a garden grows.

Minutes vanish, as crumbs take flight,
Each bite a joy, a tasty delight.
Time slips by, like melted cheese,
Who needs a watch? Just pass the peas!

Chewing Through Chapters

Books piled high, snacks by my side,
Popcorn crunching, I take the ride.
Characters leap from the pages wide,
With chocolate treats, it's a flavorful tide.

I munch on mysteries, savor each twist,
Every chapter kissed by a sweet tryst.
Gummy bears in a plot that's dire,
Fuel for the tales that never tire.

Delicacies of Discovery

Each new taste, a wild quest,
Savory secrets, I must ingest.
Cookies whisper, and donuts call,
Through batter and glaze, I topple the wall.

Tiny morsels, a treasure map,
Finding flavors, oh what a trap!
Exploring each crunch, a giggle or two,
Adventure awaits in flavors so new!

Appetizing Adventures

Pack a bag, don't forget the munch,
Trail mix ready for our hiking hunch.
Through mountains high or valleys low,
Every snack's a story, an epic show.

Laughter echoes as cookies crumble,
In between bites, we happily jumble.
The journey is rich, with each tasty round,
In the world of snacks, joy can be found!

Flavor Trails

On forks and spoons we pave our way,
With every bite, we dance and sway.
Through chocolate streams and cheese-filled roads,
Our hearts grow light, our laughter explodes.

Pickles and pies, oh what a sight,
Each crunch and munch brings pure delight.
Forget the prize at journey's end,
It's all about the snacks we send.

Midway Treats

At the fair, oh what a spree,
Cotton candy calls to me.
With corn dogs swinging on a stick,
We laugh and chow, it's quite the trick.

The carousel turns, our bellies churn,
For nachos next, it's our turn to yearn.
Through deep-fried wonders, we dash around,
With every bite, joy's easily found.

Sips and Surprises

Lemonade waves in the summer air,
Each sip brings smiles, who can compare?
With bubble teas and fizzy drinks,
We laugh until our goodness blinks.

A splash of soda, a twist of lime,
As we sip through moments, feeling sublime.
The fun isn't found in just a toast,
But in all the sips, we love the most.

Morsels of Memory

In grandma's kitchen, the smells delight,
Cookies baking in the soft twilight.
With chocolate chips that melt and ooze,
Each crumb a memory, never to lose.

Peanut butter hugs and jelly slips,
Sticky fingers and silly quips.
It's not the feast but the fun we seek,
In every morsel, laughter speaks.

The Graze of Time

In the pantry I find my glee,
A kingdom of treats calls to me.
Chips and cookies, a crunchy song,
In flavor's embrace, I can't go wrong.

My journey's not measured by miles,
But by the snacks that bring me smiles.
Each nibble a treasure, sweet or savory,
With every bite, I feel so brave and wavy.

Midnight Snacks Under Stars

Moonlight dances on my plate,
With popcorn clouds, I celebrate.
Stars twinkle like chocolate sprinkles,
While I munch, the galaxy crinkles.

Cereal serenades my late-night quest,
Each crunch a story, my very best.
In this buffet of life, I roam,
Finding joy in every nibble, my comfort zone.

Travel's Tasty Trenchers

In every city, a food map leads,
Past bakeries, where my heart feeds.
A taco truck or sushi bite,
Every stop a new delight!

I pack my bags with snacks galore,
Granola bars, and so much more.
On this journey, I drift and sail,
With taste sensations, I shall prevail.

Grazing Through Life

With a sprinkle of cheese, and a dash of fun,
I'm grazing through life, and oh what a run!
Fruits and dips, a colorful feast,
In every morsel, my joy is unleashed.

Carrots and hummus, a healthful regale,
Chocolate-covered dreams, I can't ever fail.
As I munch and I crunch, I savor the ride,
In this tasty adventure, I'm filled with pride.

Gratitude for Each Bite

In the kitchen, I take my stand,
Whisking up sweetness, oh so grand!
Chocolate chip cookies, warm and bright,
A sprinkled joy at every bite.

Cookies crumble, elevating cheer,
While munching on popcorn without a fear.
Taste the laughter, all flavors collide,
Savoring treats with spirits so wide.

Texture of the Trail

Crunchy granola on a sunny hike,
Each chew's a laugh, oh what a spike!
Mixing in berries, oh so divine,
Snackin' through nature, life's perfect line.

Trail mix heroes, a nomad's delight,
Nuts and raisins, munching in flight.
Every crunch tells a tale so bold,
Riding the trails until stories unfold.

The Candyland of Choices

Gumdrops glisten in the candy store,
Cupcakes call out, always wanting more.
Lollipops spinning, colors so bright,
Sugar highs dance through the night.

Chocolate rivers, a sweet retreat,
Marshmallow clouds, fluffy and neat.
Through the land of treats, let's take a ride,
On this sugary journey, joy can't hide.

Edible Milestones

Every birthday, a cake so tall,
Frosting rivers, let's eat it all!
Anniversary pies, passion in each slice,
Baking our memories, oh so nice.

Graduation parties, snacks galore,
The joy we share, we always adore.
Each nibble marks a moment so fine,
In the banquet of snacks, our lives intertwine.

Little Luxuries of the Journey

On the road with chips in hand,
Every stop feels like a grandstand.
With a laugh, we sip our sodas wide,
These little treasures make the ride.

Gummy bears in a crinkly bag,
Each one a delight, no reason to flag.
A snack attack in the middle of the lane,
We munch and crunch, forget the disdain.

Cookies crumble, laughter erupts,
In car seats, we're all just pups.
Sprinkled doughnuts, icing galore,
Mmm, add another, who could ignore?

So while routes may twist and turn,
It's the treats we cherish, no need to yearn.
Adventure awaits, with a snack-filled flair,
We savor each bite, without a care.

Comforts in Crunchy Moments

In the middle of nowhere, we take a break,
With a picnic of flavors, let's celebrate.
Cheese puffs giggle, popcorn bounces high,
Each little crunch says, 'Give it a try!'

Trail mix treasures keep spirits bright,
With every handful, it feels just right.
Who knew raisins could bring such delight?
In this moment, we're soaring in flight.

Sipping soda, we pass the time,
Licking fingers in a rhythm and rhyme.
Candy bars wrapped like dreams in foil,
With every bite, the laughter will boil.

So let the miles roll beneath our feet,
With sugary joy that's oh-so-sweet.
It's not just the place that we roam,
But the snacks we enjoy that make it our home.

Journey of Tasty Bites

On this road, the treats will call,
Chocolate bars and chips for all.
With every stop, a snack arises,
Each bite a burst of sweet surprises.

Lurking near every winding turn,
There's popcorn popping, and we yearn.
For ice cream cones and crispy fries,
In this adventure, joy multiplies.

So let's not rush, let's take it slow,
With every nibble, let laughter grow.
A cookie crumb or two to share,
Turns every moment into a fair.

As we wander, the flavors blend,
With gummy bears around each bend.
It's not the miles upon our feet,
But every couple of bites we eat.

Culinary Detours

Detours lead to pickle jars,
Where sour meets a world of stars.
In every taqueria we find,
A fiesta for the taste buds, so kind.

Chips and salsa, a simple spread,
With guacamole, we're easily fed.
Each stop's a feast, a quirky game,
In this snack quest, we stake our claim.

We'll stray from highways, take the lanes,
For cheesecake slices or spicy grains.
With every plate, we chant and cheer,
Each savory bite, we hold so dear.

So pack your bags, let's hit the road,
With soda cans and pizza load.
For every twist in this fun ride,
It's the snacks we find that take us wide.

Savoring Every Crumb

A crumb falls softly, hear the cheer,
As donuts glisten, they draw near.
With frosting colors bold and bright,
Each nibble sends our hearts in flight.

Popcorn kernels, light as air,
With every crunch, we have a flair.
Nachos stacked with cheesy dreams,
This journey's sweeter than it seems.

Let's slow it down, unwrap the treat,
When cookies call, we can't retreat.
In bursts of flavor, laughter thrives,
A tasty trail where joy derives.

So grab a fork or take a bite,
With every moment, we feel light.
In the grand swerve of taste we chase,
It's crumbles shared that fill the space.

The Sweetness of Each Moment

In every moment, taste and play,
With candy bars that lead the way.
A sprinkle here, a drizzle there,
Life's sweeter when we pause and share.

Cupcakes rising, a work of art,
Sugary smiles that warm the heart.
As we giggle over flavors bold,
The treats we chase make stories told.

With marshmallow fluff and cookie dough,
Our laughter paves the way to go.
Each bite we take, a memory spun,
In every stop, we find the fun.

So take a seat, let's dig right in,
To bowls of joy where we begin.
And in each crunch, let's raise a toast,
To snacks we love, the ones we boast.

Tasting Moments Along the Way

When we wander, bags in hand,
With treats to munch, we take a stand.
Each breadcrumb left, a tale to tell,
Of savory bites, we know so well.

Lemon drops and chocolate bars,
Snack attacks beneath the stars.
With every crunch, a laugh we share,
In the quirky moments, we declare.

So many roads, with tastings near,
Potato chips and laughter, dear.
With every bite, a journey found,
In flavors sweet, our joy unbound.

Savoring the Side Trails

On winding paths, oh what a spree,
Where gummy bears hang from a tree!
Cookies frolic in the breeze,
As we munch on snacks with such ease.

In sunlit spots, we spread our cheer,
Beneath the shade, our snacks appear.
A rippled crisp, a fizzy sip,
The happiest of picnics, oh what a trip!

Each twist and turn holds a delight,
With popcorn dreams that take to flight.
In every nibble, stories wake,
Our merry band, we laugh and shake.

In Praise of Picnic Packs

Oh, picnic packs, we lift our toast,
In every layer, we find the most.
From sandwiches to fruit galore,
Each bite an adventure we can't ignore.

Thermos filled with soup so warm,
A brownie cozy, a gusty charm.
With blankets spread on grassy floors,
We munch and giggle, our hearts explore.

Chips crumble with each jump and shout,
While ants parade, we just laugh out loud.
In the great outdoors, we celebrate,
With every bite, a twist of fate.

The Sweetness of Every Turn

Around the bend, a donut shop,
Where sprinkles rain, we simply stop.
A pastry here, a snack attack,
Every journey's twist just pulls us back.

So grab a cone, embrace the ride,
With cookies close as tour guides.
In laughter sweet, we toast our snacks,
With every bite, we never lack.

So here's to joy in every taste,
A treasure trail, not a moment waste.
For in the munching, we often find,
The sweetest memories left behind.

Spice of the Road

On highways wide, we roam and roam,
With bags of chips, our snack-time home.
Laughter spills, as crumbs cascade,
Adventure's sweet, when snacks are made.

The candy aisle calls, can't resist,
A gummy bear? We can't coexist!
A soda pop explodes with glee,
In sticky hands, we feel so free.

Granola bars, the perfect fuel,
Each bite we take, we break the rule.
Driving slow, we savor each,
The taste is grand, that's what we preach!

So pack your treats and hit the road,
For tasty joys are ours to load.
Each mile we munch, a giggle shared,
In every crunch, we know we dared.

A Feast for the Feet

Flip-flops slapping, we take a stride,
Chasing sunsets, with snacks as our guide.
Trail mix upped in pockets deep,
With popcorn stashed, who needs to sleep?

The journey's long, so bring your bite,
Chocolate bars will make it right.
Legs are tired, but spirits rise,
As french fries dance beneath the skies.

Each path we walk, a feast untold,
With jellybeans, our hearts unfold.
Anticipation builds with every crunch,
Filling up for that giant lunch.

Adventure awaits on every heel,
With snacks, the fun is all too real.
So lace your shoes, and run with flair,
For every journey has snacks to share.

Chew on This

Beneath the sun, we munch away,
Marshmallow fluff to brighten the day.
Peanut butter smudged on fingers,
Our laughter echoes, the fun lingers.

A road trip game? Let's make it sweet,
Who can guess the next snack treat?
With every bite, our spirits soar,
Tacos and chips, we always ask for more.

The cookie jar's the true delight,
With chocolate chips, we take our bite.
Lollipops swirl in rainbow hues,
In quirky hats, we share the news.

So grab a friend, share your stash,
With giggles loud and snacks that smash.
In every chew, we feel the bliss,
A recipe for fun—let's not miss!

Flavorful Footprints

Footprints marked with crumbs of joy,
Each step a snack, we can't destroy.
Candy wrappers litter the way,
Reminding us of all the play.

Banana peels on slippery roads,
We giggle as we dodge the loads.
Those gooey sweets, a sticky fate,
With laughter shared, we celebrate.

Sugar rush on every trail,
As giggly tales begin to sail.
With potato chips and juicy bites,
Every meal transforms our sights.

So let's explore, with snacks in hand,
Every twist and turn, oh so grand.
For every crunch is pure delight,
In tasty journeys, we ignite.

Nature's Snack Bar

In the forest, munching leaves,
Squirrels race with playful thieves.
Between the trees, a picnic spreads,
Crumbs and giggles mark our threads.

Mushrooms peek from under frost,
Gathered snacks are never lost.
Berries sweet, with laughter mix,
Nature's treats, a tasty fix.

Ants in queue for crumbs they yearn,
Every morsel, we discern.
Crackers served on a leaf plate,
Only smiles on this fine date.

Raindrops dance on juicy fruit,
A feast for all, no need to hoot.
Nature struts her snack parade,
In this buffet, we gladly wade.

Sweet Serenades of the Sky

Clouds like marshmallows drifting high,
Cotton candy dreams fly by.
Sugar sprinkles on the breeze,
Giggles grow like honeybees.

Stars at dusk, like chocolate chips,
Whisper tales of sugary trips.
Pies of starlight in the night,
Taste the joy, it feels so right.

Lemonade clouds, a zesty grin,
Dancing raindrops, let's begin!
Feasting on the joyful sights,
Skyward snacks give pure delight.

So grab a wink from the moon's glow,
In this treat, our spirits grow.
Every twinkle, every spark,
Sweet serenades, we leave our mark.

Tasty Trails and Tales

On winding paths, we find our snacks,
Trail mix giggles in our packs.
Granola bars and laughter shared,
With every step, our joy declared.

Fruits along the way, so bright,
Chasing down the fading light.
Peppermint leaves and berry smiles,
Winding roads stretch on for miles.

Each crunchy bite tells a tale,
Of silly slips and joyous trails.
Cookies hidden in the grass,
With every nibble, moments pass.

So let us wander, snack in hand,
Through forests wild and golden sand.
With tasty trails, and tales to weave,
In every snack, we'll never leave.

Marzipan Musings

In a world where sweets collide,
Marzipan dreams become our guide.
Figures dancing, made of paste,
Sugar-coated, never haste.

Candy castles in the sun,
Every bite begins the fun.
With smiles shaped in sugary dreams,
The chocolate river gently gleams.

Frosted thoughts on a cake parade,
Insatiable, we'll never fade.
With every chew, our hearts expand,
Together, munching hand in hand.

Whisk away on sugary sails,
Joyful stories cushioned in bales.
In a marzipan world, we thrive,
Where sweet creations come alive.

Zesty Twists of Fate

In a world of crispy bites,
Chasing cheese and spicy nights.
Grab a handful, take a chance,
Life's a party, join the dance!

Potato chips and ice cream cones,
Happy grins and crunchy tones.
Lemon drops and pickles sweet,
Flip the script, indulge that treat!

Burgers stacked and pies galore,
Every taste just opens doors.
Doughnut dreams and all things fried,
Let your cravings be your guide!

So let's toast to every bite,
Each snack a little pure delight.
Forget the journey, just enjoy,
A chip, a dip – oh, what a joy!

Sips of Serenity

With every sip, the world gets bright,
Chocolate milkshakes take their flight.
Strawberry fizz and lemon splash,
Chill with snacks, oh, such a bash!

Fruit punch smiles and cookie dough,
Life's a breeze, just let it flow.
Twirling twizzlers, bubblegum dreams,
Sip by sip, laugh till it seems!

Refreshments sweet, giggles galore,
Chasing flavors, who could ask for more?
Mix it up, add some flair,
Every moment, joy to share!

Raise your glass, toast to fun,
With every sip, we've just begun.
Savoring laughs and snacks, oh my!
Cheers to the treats that make us fly!

Munching Through Milestones

Stepping stones of pretzel bites,
Celebrate with crunchy sights.
Birthday cake and nacho cheese,
Every crunch brings us to our knees!

Milestone munchies, sweet and vast,
Each one gone, we have a blast.
Caramel popcorn, oh so fine,
Mark the moments, sip the wine!

With nachos piled like our dreams,
Joy erupts in cheesy beams.
Celebrate each tasty treat,
Milestones made with every bite we eat!

So let's munch through every phase,
In laughter's glow, we spend our days.
Snacks unite, bonds they create,
Chomp away, it's never late!

Cooked Dreams In Motion

In the kitchen, pot starts to dance,
Simmering warmth, let's take a chance.
Flavors blend like a wild affair,
Cooked creations fill the air!

Pasta twirls in marinara bliss,
With every bite, we steal a kiss.
Batch of cookies, golden brown,
Sweet aroma, never a frown!

From sizzling pans to grilled delights,
Chili dogs on starry nights.
Whisking dreams with each delight,
Cooked paths lit with tasty light!

So spoon each moment, savor and laugh,
In the buffet of life, we find our path.
Stir the pot, let flavors show,
Every key ingredient? Just go with the flow!

Nourishment on the Path

On the trail of dreams we roam,
With chips and cookies, we make our home.
A granola bar sings sweet delight,
While gummy bears dance in the light.

As we wander, we munch and chew,
Finding flavors, oh so true.
Popcorn pops with a joyous sound,
In every step, a crunch is found.

With sandwiches packed and laughs to share,
Every bite shows how much we care.
Pickles and peanuts in the mix,
Fueling our journey with little tricks.

So let's snack on this silly spree,
Laughter and munching, just you and me.
For every journey that we take,
Is spiced with snacks that make us shake.

Whispers of Flavor

The road ahead is paved with fries,
A joyful feast beneath the skies.
A slice of pie and cheesy flair,
With every bite, we strip despair.

Chocolate bars whisper in my ear,
"Join the party, have no fear!"
Soda fountains bubble and froth,
As we snack our way through the sloth.

Each trail we stroll, a smorgasbord,
Of nature's goodies, we can hoard.
So grab your snacks, we've much to munch,
Our taste buds sing with every crunch.

Rays of sun and laughter spread,
With pretzel twists and popcorn led.
Let's savor each tasty delight,
In our hearts, it's pure delight.

Footprints and Flavors

As I walk along this winding path,
I nibble chips, I share a laugh.
Trail mix spills, oh what a mess,
But snackin' hard is no distress!

With jellybeans and ice cream cones,
We dance on pathways made of stones.
The journey's sweet and sometimes rough,
But snacks make everything more tough.

Each bite a step, each crunch a cheer,
Potato chips, bring out the good cheer!
Through every twist and every turn,
For snacks we crave, our hearts do yearn.

So grab a burger, hold it tight,
With every snack, our joy takes flight.
Though footprints fade on this old track,
The snacks and giggles bring us back.

Gusto in the Journey

With every step, I munch and sway,
A candy bar to save the day.
Nachos crunch with every laugh,
Filling our hearts and our photograph.

Slurping sodas, we glide and zoom,
Snack attacks brighten every room.
Popcorn balls and doughnuts galore,
Each sugary bite begs for more!

On this trip, let's feast and play,
With cookie dough leading the way.
Every savory moment is pure bliss,
With each bite taken, we'll chase the abyss.

So let's celebrate with laughter and cheer,
Munching memories year after year.
In every giggle, in every crunch,
We find our joy with every lunch.

Bites on the Path

Walking down the winding lane,
Fumbling with my bag of grains.
Crackers crunch and chips do squeak,
Every snack's a joyful streak.

Each step brings a new delight,
Chocolate bars that make me bright.
Peanut butter, oh so sweet,
Life, it seems, is quite a treat.

Fruits are rolling down the hill,
Gummy bears that bring a thrill.
Pizza slices on the go,
Wonderful things to savor slow.

So let's crunch through every hour,
With tasty bites, we'll feel the power.
In this feast, we'll laugh and play,
Let's munch our cares right away!

Harvesting Joys of the Journey

In the basket of sweet delight,
Cookies winking in the light.
Donuts dancing, round and bright,
Nibble here, life feels just right.

Every nibble tells a tale,
Of savory dreams that never pale.
Chips and salsa, crunchy zing,
Join me now, together we sing!

Pickles popping in their jar,
Trail mix cheering from afar.
Each little bite a giggle sound,
In this journey, joy is found.

From sweet to savory, it's all grand,
Even veggies lend a hand.
Harvest smiles with every munch,
Let's enjoy this tasty brunch!

Pastries of the Present

Pies and cakes all stacked so high,
With frosting dreams that touch the sky.
Croissants whisper sweet and flaky,
Each bite makes my heart feel shaky.

Tarts adorned with fruity charms,
Lifting spirits, spreading balms.
Brownies beckon from the plate,
Chocolates tease, it's never late.

Bakers laugh as they create,
Treats that simply can't wait.
Sprinkles jump, confetti flies,
In this moment, joy multiplies.

Pastries beckon, join the fun,
With every nibble, we have won.
Savor now, let worries part,
These little bites, they steal your heart!

Whispers of Delightful Snacks

In the pantry, treasures hide,
With every crinkle, dreams collide.
Chips are rustling, cookies sigh,
Muffins giggle, oh my, my!

Popcorn pops like tiny folks,
Making merry with their jokes.
Brownies whisper, "Have a taste!"
Life's a feast, not one to waste.

Jellybeans in colors bright,
Filling days with pure delight.
Every snack tells tales anew,
Munching smiles just like a crew.

So let's gather, share a laugh,
In a world of snacks, we craft.
With every bite, joy's on the rise,
Here's to snacks, the great surprise!

Chasing Cravings

In search of glory, we rush around,
With cookies calling, we'll be spellbound.
Chasing sweetness, oh what a race,
Yet we stumble in our snack-filled embrace.

To munch or not, as crumbs fall down,
We debate choices with a goofy frown.
Chocolate or chips, a serious plight,
But laughter erupts, as we munch and bite.

Picnic Philosophies

A blanket spread beneath the sun,
Sandwiches talk, 'Come join the fun!'
With lemonade laughter, we sip and cheer,
Debates on pizza bring everyone near.

The ants hold court, such tiny foes,
Friendly bickering over fries and prose.
Chips fly high in the playful fray,
Philosophers snacking on this fine day.

Delightful Diversions

In the pantry's depths, treasures await,
Popcorn laughs, tossing kernels of fate.
We dance with pretzels, all twist and shout,
Finding joy in what snacking's about.

Gumdrops giggle, so brightly they tease,
While gummy bears weave tales with ease.
Each bite's a journey on a tasty quest,
We relish each moment, feeling so blessed.

The Essence of Each Bite

Every cracker holds a secret delight,
And cheese with its humor shines ever bright.
We savor each crunch, each bubbling laugh,
Finding joy in snacks that make us daft.

When cookies crumble, we still grin wide,
For crumbs are just proof of the fun inside.
Delicious detours lead us astray,
Yet we wouldn't have it another way.

Grazing Through the Hours

In every nook, there lies a treat,
The crunch of chips beneath my feet.
A chocolate bar, my trusty guide,
On this plush sofa, I confide.

With popcorn clouds that float up high,
I take the leap, I'll snack and fly.
Forget the plans and what's ahead,
These little bites, my life, it thread.

With dips and spreads in joyful glee,
I dance around so carefree.
Each cookie crumbles like my stress,
In snacks, I find my happiness.

So here's a toast, let laughter flow,
To munch and crunch—let's steal the show!
Adventures await in every bite,
Together we snack, from morn to night.

Snack-Sized Revelations

In the cupboard, secrets hide,
A sweet surprise, oh what a ride!
With chips and salsa side by side,
My taste buds dance, they cannot bide.

With every nibble, wisdom's shared,
A gummy bear, none compared!
The kettle pops, a joyful tune,
While brownie bites cause me to swoon.

In every package, stories flow,
Of salty crunch and sugar's glow.
The clock ticks down, but I won't fret,
For snacks, my friend, are my safety net.

So let's indulge, let's feast and play,
With each tasty morsel, brighter day.
We'll snack our way through life's big show,
With every bite, our hearts will grow.

Palate and Passage

A cart rolls in, let's fill it fast,
With tasty treats, a hearty blast.
From nachos piled up just right,
To berries that catch the sunlight.

Through each aisle, I roam with glee,
In search of goodness, just for me.
A fizzy drink, a donut dash,
Each snack, a thrill, a joyous splash.

With every crunch, a journey starts,
To flavor lands and happy hearts.
No rush to go, just munch away,
The snacks will guide, they're here to stay.

Embrace the taste, the fun unfolds,
In crispy bites or marshmallow molds.
Together we munch, let's raise a cheer,
For every snack brings us near!

Indulgence in Motion

On bumpy roads, I find my glee,
With wrappers crinkling next to me.
A cookie jar that shakes and rolls,
With snacks in arms, it's how I stroll.

The windy path, it calls my name,
But popcorn calls me just the same.
Through bridges crossed and hills I climb,
My heart is full—snack time's sublime!

Each journey made is filled with zest,
Each juicy bite, I must confess.
So on I munch, with joy in sight,
With every snack, the world feels bright.

Embracing all of flavor's joy,
A chocolate bar, my soul's convoy.
Let's laugh and snack and feel alive,
With every chew, we truly thrive.

Morsels in the Moonlight

Under the glow of starry skies,
Chips and dip in cosmic guise,
Gazing at the milky way,
Finding snacks leads us astray.

Laughter fills the midnight air,
Popcorn kernels everywhere,
Counting bites of cheesy puffs,
The night is good, but snacks are tough.

Marshmallows toast on fiery beams,
Sweetness flows in gooey dreams,
With every crunch, we share a lore,
Under the moon, we crave for more.

So here's to journeys, not the score,
But to treasures we can't ignore,
In every pit stop, each quick snack,
We pile the joy, then head back!

The Hidden Treats of Travel

Packing bags and checking lists,
Forgetting snacks, oh, what a twist,
Roadside burger drives us mad,
But fries and shakes make us glad.

Map in hand, we take a chance,
Will it lead to a snack-filled romance?
From candy stores to food carts near,
Each bite becomes a path so dear.

Beneath a bridge, a taco truck,
Bowls of salsa—wish us luck!
As laughter rings, the flavors blend,
Treasures found around each bend.

So while the journey's paved with grit,
It's snacks that give the sweetest wit,
For every mile, a tasty find,
In every crunch, our hearts unwind!

Finding Flavor in Wanderlust

With suitcase packed and spirit high,
Off we go, just you and I,
To sample treats both strange and new,
A world of flavors waits for you.

Let's skip the sights, just grab a bite,
Treats that sparkle, pure delight,
From gelato by the seaside,
To crispy chips with jokes inside.

Every market holds a dream,
Munching pastries, sipping cream,
And as we taste, we start to roam,
In every nibble, we find a home.

Oh, how the map delights the palate,
From sweet to savory, we'll not stall it,
So here's to snacks, they guide our quest,
In every crunch, we find our zest!

The Delicacies of Discovery

Adventurers of every age,
Hunting snacks from page to page,
Through cities bright and forests deep,
Where every flavor makes us leap.

With every turn, we snugly bite,
Candies come, and cookies light,
As waterfalls may swirl and flow,
It's nachos that steal the show.

Maps are drawn in chocolate stains,
Our hearts beat fast like sugar rains,
In fancy shops and humble stalls,
Taste buds dance as each one calls.

So as we search for what is grand,
It's treats that make this journey planned,
For travelers with quickened pace,
Snack in hand is where we embrace!

Bites of Bliss

In moments sweet, we take a bite,
With chocolate treats, our hearts ignite.
A journey shared with snacks so fine,
Each crumb a memory, each nibble divine.

Instead of maps, we check our meals,
With every snack, our laughter feels.
A chip, a dip, a candy fling,
In joyous chaos, our taste buds sing.

Forget the road, it's what we munch,
A spicy wing, a crispy crunch.
With every sip, the world's a laugh,
In this snack quest, we find the path.

So raise a toast, to popcorn nights,
To nachos, cookies, pizza bites.
In every sip and every crunch,
We savor life—so let's munch a bunch!

To Taste Each Mile

With every step, a treat awaits,
A donut's glaze, it's never late.
On this great path, we snack and glide,
Exploring flavors, side by side.

From fizzy drinks to cheesy fries,
Adventures bloom beneath the skies.
As we wander, snacks at hand,
Each tasty stop is simply grand.

The journey's joy, it peaks and dips,
With pepperoni on our lips.
In every spot, we feast and play,
Tasting life along the way.

So let's map out a route of fun,
Where nachos spark and cupcakes run.
For every mile, a crunch we'll share,
With buddies close, without a care!

Textures of Experience

A crinkly bag, a soft delight,
The shadows dance in snack-time light.
Each flavor tells a tale anew,
Of cheesy puffs and barbecue.

Nibbles offer tales untold,
As gummy worms partake in bold.
In crispy hosts, adventure glows,
Unfolding joy in food that flows.

With every crunch, we find our way,
A journey sweet throughout the day.
Popcorn's fluff and chocolate's swirl,
In this banquet, we twirl and whirl.

So scratch that map, just grab a bite,
To savor moments, oh what a sight.
For textures bring us all delight,
In tasty realms, our spirits flight!

Cravings Along the Way

With every mile, the cravings rise,
A burger here, beneath the skies.
Hot fries calling, "Join the feast!"
In each new place, we snack the least.

From candy shops to taco stalls,
Each stop we make, a siren calls.
A fizzy drink, a chocolate bar,
With each delight, we wander far.

So cheer for chips and brownies, too,
In every dip, we find our crew.
With laughter shared and goodies shared,
In this grand trip, we are well paired.

Let's roam with treats that spark the fun,
In each sweet bite, we come undone.
It's not the miles but what we taste,
These munchy moments, never waste!

Relishing the Reroutes

Traveling the winding road,
With a picnic basket full,
Lost but never lonely,
Snack breaks are quite the pull.

Map out a route with glee,
But find a place to munch,
Each detour tastes better,
Especially when you crunch!

Through jungles of junk food,
With chips that always crack,
A sandwich sings a song,
Making reroutes smack back!

So wander off the path,
In flavors we'll invest,
Each journey is a feast,
Life's a snack-bursting fest!

The Taste of Today

Wake up and smell the toast,
Crispy crusts are grand,
Today's feast comes alive,
With butter at hand.

Coffee brews like magic,
A caffeine gush ascent,
Sipping on a joy shot,
My taste is heaven-sent.

Lunch rolls in with laughter,
Pizza slices grin wide,
Toppings dance on crusts,
They take me for a ride.

Dinner brings its charm,
With a salad's joyful crunch,
Every bite a giggle,
In this tasty punch!

Fragrant Memories on the Trail

Hiking up the hills today,
I packed some snacks so bright,
Granola bars like treasure,
A sweet and savory sight.

The trail whispers of popcorn,
Pine trees scent the air,
Each crunch a treasured echo,
Nature's culinary flair.

A trail mix of pure delight,
M&Ms and nuts collide,
Every nibble bursts with joy,
A snack pack on my side.

These moments, oh so chewy,
Through laughter and a crunch,
The memories we harvest,
In every happy munch!

Appetizing Anecdotes

Gather round for stories,
As chips begin to fly,
Dips dive into laughter,
With salsa on the sly.

A tale of big burritos,
That almost slipped away,
But we caught it with our mouths,
A taco Tuesday bouquet!

The chocolate cake of legends,
Had a frosting scandal,
By the time it hit the table,
It was gone like a candle!

So raise your glasses high,
To snacks that stole the show,
In the stories that we share,
They're the stars, you know!

Culinary Crossroads

At every fork, a snack appears,
A crispy treat to calm my fears.
Beneath the stars, I munch and crunch,
With cheesy puffs, I make my lunch.

I wander through this edible maze,
With chocolate trails that ever amaze.
Each twist and turn, a tasty quest,
Popcorn mountains, oh what a fest!

A soda stream, my trusty guide,
As candy waves crash, I glide.
To savory shores, I dip and dive,
With every bite, I feel alive.

So here I am, with treats galore,
At every stop, there's so much more.
Each tasty laugh, a sprinkle of fun,
In this snackland, I've already won!

Savor the Scenic Route

The road is long, with chips in hand,
A picnic spread upon the sand.
With every view, I take a bite,
My journey's snacks bring pure delight.

Donuts glazed like morning sun,
With every mile, I taste the fun.
Fruit baskets tossed on grassy knolls,
A gourmet plan, it fills my rolls.

A burger with a side of fries,
The open road beneath blue skies.
Each morsel pops like laughter loud,
In this buffet, I feel so proud.

So here's to travels with treats to share,
Days filled with flavors beyond compare.
As I roam, let the baking start,
A snack-filled journey, close to my heart!

Journey with Flavor

On this adventure, I find my place,
In every bite, I see a face.
With gummy bears, we sing and dance,
While macaroons lead the romance.

A road of nachos, salsa bright,
And popcorn rivers, such a sight!
Each candy bar is like a friend,
On this crisp path, it's never end.

With every meal, a story told,
Spicing life with flavors bold.
Crackers and cheese steal the show,
In this life feast, there's room to grow.

So let's toast to snacks we adore,
With every crunch, I crave for more.
In this journey, joy quickly flows,
To savor snacks, wherever it goes!

The Crumbs of Yesterday

In the rearview, crumbs that fall,
Remnants of snacks, my greatest haul.
A donut dream with icing spills,
Echoes of laughter, the heart fulfills.

Pop-tart memories, sweet and bright,
As I remember that last bite.
A cookie giggle, moments shared,
In every crumb, my soul was bared.

Chocolate trails that spun around,
In this past road, joy is found.
Every flavor brings a smile,
Let's munch on down this tasty mile.

So here's to crumbs and tales they weave,
A snack-filled past, I still believe.
Collecting flavors, like stars at night,
Each one a memory, pure delight!

The Appetizer of Adventure

With every step we take, we munch,
A tiny piece of pie, a little crunch.
From pies to fries, the tastes unfold,
Every bite a story, brave and bold.

A journey starts with chips and dip,
Oh look, there's cake, let's take a trip!
Between each giggle, and silly snack,
We find our joy, and never look back.

Tales are shared with popcorn flair,
As we travel light, without a care.
On a road less traveled, nutrition comes,
With every stop, we laugh, it hums.

So grab your fork and let us feign,
A savory quest of joyous gain!
Through bites and sips, we light the way,
In every morsel, our laughter stays.

Flavors Between the Steps

In life's little stroll, we stop to graze,
On gummy bears and sun-kissed rays.
Every bite a twist, a zesty treat,
As we venture on, our hearts skip a beat.

Chocolate bars and salty nuts,
Make each brave step feel quite the strut.
With jelly beans and jellyfish dreams,
Our path's not empty; it's bursting at the seams.

A rainbow of snacks, we'll take a cue,
As we laugh with friends, and sip some brew.
Between hot dogs and sweet cotton candy,
Our trials turn sweet, and life feels dandy.

So pack your lunch; let's make it wild,
With sprinkles of joy, we're every child.
In friendship and snacks, we place our bets,
With flavors unbound, no regrets, no debts.

A Feast of Experiences

With every morsel, we carve our way,
Through jelly rolls and a rich souffle.
The more we taste, the more we find,
A banquet for the heart and mind.

Biting into laughter, munching on cheer,
It's the moments that count, so let's draw near.
With pop rocks and cookie dough dreams,
Our palette of life bursts at the seams.

As we take a stroll for a quick bite,
A cupcake detour feels quite right.
With every crunch, a story shared,
Over nachos, we never feel scared.

So gather 'round, let's feast and cheer,
With flavors so bright, our hearts sincere.
Each snack a nugget of joy we've caught,
In this banquet of memories, we've fought.

Snacks from the Heart

In the family van, we snack and chat,
Potato chips and a cozy hat.
The roads twist and turn, but that's okay,
For every snack eats our worries away.

Gummies shaped like cars, it's quite the ride,
As we giggle and munch with arms spread wide.
With milkshakes swirling, we feel so free,
Each sip of joy just adds to glee.

Every table spread, a tapestry spun,
Of homemade delights and laughter, oh, what fun!
With every fried bite, we share our hearts,
Around the big table, where laughter starts.

So let's toast with snacks, our spirits rise,
For it's the moments that bring the prize.
In this journey together, we surely know,
The snacks of our hearts will always glow.

The Crunch Beneath Our Feet

With each step, there's a crack, a crunch,
Potato chips and pretzels in a tasty bunch.
We wander along, munching with glee,
One bite of joy, who needs a decree?

The trail may be long, but snacks are the prize,
Gummies and popcorn dancing before our eyes.
Every pathway leads to a flavorful treat,
Tickling our taste buds, life's little feat.

So here we go, on this whimsical ride,
With a trail mix chaser and chips as our guide.
Forget the grand view, it's the nibbles we seek,
Snack-sational smiles beam on every cheek.

In the crunch beneath our feet, we do find,
The laughter and joy that colors our mind.
For travel's not lonely, we cheerfully spat,
In the crumbs and the chips, we happily chat.

Savory Stories of the Road

As we travel the roads, tales are spun,
Muffins and candies, oh what fun!
Pepperoni rolls tell of places afar,
While bags of popcorn shine like a star.

Every pit stop brings a new yarn to tell,
Salsa and chips, it's a party we dwell.
With each little munch, our laughter will grow,
Snacking on memories, where else would we go?

The sandwiches packed, a deck of delights,
With cookies and cakes for our daytime bites.
A sprinkle of laughter, a dash of good cheer,
The road fills with flavors, everything's here.

So grab your snacks, let the stories unfold,
With each savory bite, a memory pure gold.
We've ventured so far, not just miles we've roamed,
It's in every bite that our heart finds its home.

Gourmet Footprints

As we march on this path, oh what a treat,
Gourmet delights and sugary sweets.
Each step's a new flavor, a crispy delight,
Biting our way into culinary night.

With cheesy crackers and chocolate bars,
Our footsteps echo like tasty guitars.
Forget maps and signs, it's the snacks that we trace,
In this culinary journey, we've found our place.

From donut shops bright to taco stands bold,
Each morsel a story, a memory untold.
As we dance through the aisles of each vibrant store,
Our stomachs like guides, always yearning for more.

So follow the crumbs, let them lead the way,
To new snacking adventures, let's laugh and play.
For in every connection, each delicious bite,
We savor the journey, everything feels right.

A Journey Seasoned

On this journey we spice as we weave,
Chips and salsa, oh, we won't grieve.
Every mile is seasoned with snacks and cheer,
With cookies and fizzy drinks always near.

Like popcorn popping with a joyous sound,
We snack away worries as we roam around.
Nourishing smiles with a dash of delight,
Each tasty morsel feels perfectly right.

With wraps and dips, we feast on the trails,
Every bite tells us those savory tales.
As laughter drips like butter on the corn,
We wander united, and happily worn.

So gather your snacks, let's set out to roam,
With flavors as friends, we'll find our way home.
The journey's not measured in time, oh no,
It's the size of our smiles and how much we know.

Sweet Stops Along the Way

On this road of sugar dreams,
We halt for creamy swirls and creams.
Chocolate rivers, honey flows,
Every mile more sweetly glows.

A donut shop, a bakery's charm,
Each bite a hug, each treat a balm.
Sprinkles dance like confetti bright,
In the land of sugar, everything's right.

Cupcakes sing with frosting grace,
Sugar rush takes us to space.
Laughter bubbles, a sticky mess,
In frosting skirts, we find our zest.

So here we munch, so here we play,
With sweet delights along the way.
Our journey's joy is wrapped in dough,
As we snack and giggle, off we go!

Tangy Tales of the Trail

On the path where pickles loom,
Zesty flavors chase the gloom.
We pop a tart, we twist a lime,
Each taste a trove, each nibble sublime.

Lemons laugh as they zing and roll,
Crisp cucumbers claim their stroll.
Sour notes and giggles blend,
With every crunch, the fun won't end.

Pineapple twirls in goofy cheer,
Jellybeans bounce as we draw near.
Tart and tangy, we can't refrain,
Snack by snack, we dance through rain.

So grab a bite, come take a ride,
With zesty tales, we'll never hide.
On this trail where flavors clash,
We smile, we munch, in a delightful bash!

The Spice of Existence

Munching on life like spicy chips,
Every crispy crunch gives us quips.
Cayenne dances, and so does zest,
In this flavor fest, we feel our best.

From curry clouds to chili waves,
We dive in boldly, as the spice saves.
Paprika winks, and garlic grins,
With every bite, the joy begins.

Ginger snaps as we make our way,
Herbs and spices join our play.
Hot sauce laughter, a glorious sting,
In our pocket, the joy we bring.

So sprinkle on fun, let flavors explode,
With spices galore, let's stay in the load.
For in each mustard seed and cinnamon ride,
The essence of joy will be our guide!

Chewy Chapters of Our Quest

With every step, we grab a bite,
Gummy bears make our hearts take flight.
In chewy moments, laughter grows,
As stories come from cookie doughs.

Like taffy sticks, our joy's entwined,
Each chew a memory, sweetly combined.
From licorice lanes to popcorn peaks,
In every chew, adventure speaks.

Chocolate chews in fluffy skies,
With every pull, a new surprise.
Marshmallow dreams drift and sway,
As we munch through each glorious day.

So let's unwrap the joy we seek,
With chewy bites, let laughter peak.
In each adventure, we find our zest,
Munching through stories, feeling blessed!

Explorations with a Side of Treats

On a road where cookies reign,
Every bite's a sweet campaign.
Doughnuts dance in morning light,
Chasing snacks, we feel so right.

Laughter echoes, crumbs in tow,
Spilling chips, oh what a show!
Each flavor tells a tale so grand,
With every crunch, we take a stand.

Ice cream mountains, sprinkles rain,
Taste bud treasures, not in vain.
In this journey, joy we seek,
With salty treats and sweets so chic.

So grab your snacks, let's hit the road,
Adventure calls, a tasty code.
With giggles shared and smiles so bright,
Every stop's a pure delight.

Edible Adventures Await

Pack your bags, don't forget the fries,
To new horizons, the pizza flies.
With soda fountains and candy trails,
We'll surf on desserts, tell endless tales.

The world's a menu, come take a bite,
In search of snacks, oh what a sight!
Chocolates hiding in every nook,
Smorgasbords in every cookbook.

Forget the miles; let's map the snacks,
Tacos and nachos in giant packs.
With laughter loud and taste buds wide,
Every edible step is our joy-filled ride.

So wheel those carts, let's roll away,
To flavor towns where we can play.
Adventures tasty, let's not be late,
In the kingdom of snacks, we celebrate!

The Route Less Chewed

Take the back roads, skip the tourist traps,
Follow the scent of doughy wraps.
Burgers flipping, fries piled high,
Eating snacks as we wave goodbye.

Forget the maps, let's graze all day,
Chewy trails lead us on our way.
With candy clouds and popcorn skies,
Every snack a sweet surprise.

Skip the end, enjoy the ride,
Join hands with donuts, let them guide.
Each crunchy moment makes us grin,
In this odyssey, it's a tasty win.

So pack your appetite, roll with glee,
Every corner's a culinary spree.
With laughter served and flavors loud,
On this route, we're snackers proud.

Flavor-filled Footsteps

Step by step, we munch along,
With jellybeans as our theme song.
Peanut butter paths, sticky and sweet,
Every crunch beneath our feet.

With nachos crunching, oh what a sound,
Each tasty morsel knows no ground.
Savoring flavors, from savory to sweet,
In this adventure, we can't be beat.

Cookies crumble, laughter swells,
In between bites, we share our tales.
The road is long, snacks lead the way,
In every moment, it's a feast today.

So take a leap, embrace the fun,
Every snack means we've already won.
With flavor-filled footsteps, we will dance,
On this wild ride, let's take a chance!

Nibbles for the Road Ahead

In the suitcase, a treat or two,
Chocolate bars, chips, and goo.
Every bite brings a grin so wide,
Snack moments, our joy and pride.

Plan the route, but heart's in the crunch,
Gummy bears for that midday munch.
Pretzel sticks like little wands,
Casting spells with buttery hands.

Take a trip around the block,
Unearth delights with every tick-tock.
Popcorn popping, laughter so bright,
Adventures bloom with every bite.

So pack your bags, don't forget the fries,
Fruits and nuts, the perfect surprise.
When roads are long and time feels slow,
Nibbles transform the journey's flow.

Chewing on Memories

Every candy holds a story told,
A frosted cupcake, memories bold.
Under starry skies, laughter unfolds,
Chasing the sweetness, hearts turned gold.

Beverages fizz, like bubbles of fun,
Sunshine giggles, under the sun.
Breadsticks dipped in warmth and cheese,
Every moment, a savory tease.

Frame the memories with licorice ropes,
Share the popcorn, spark childhood hopes.
A realm of flavors, a laughable spree,
Each snack a trip down memory's sea.

Celebrate the journeys that fill our days,
With treats in hand, in whimsical ways.
For in every nibble, a tale we'll find,
A feast of laughter, a journey unconfined.

Travel Tastes Better with Snacks

Map drawn out, but joy's in the bites,
Salty chips under city lights.
With every crunch, the world feels right,
Savor the journey, from day to night.

Around the globe, or just next door,
Exploring flavors, seeking more.
Tacos, sushi, a little surprise,
With snacks in hand, each moment flies.

Sipping sodas with friends in tow,
Laughs shared like an endless flow.
For every snack is a door to roam,
Turning the road into a cozy home.

So pack your goodies, a varied spread,
Whether chips or cookies, you're well-fed.
On paths unknown, where adventure plays,
With tasty treats, we'll sing for days.

Candies for the Curious

Curious minds need sugary trails,
Candy-coated fortunes, mysterious tales.
Lollipops shining, bright as the sun,
Chocolate treasures for everyone.

Beneath the wraps, surprises await,
Gumdrops, jellybeans—all on our plate.
With every nibble, a question lingers,
Why's the sky blue? Oh, the fateful fingers.

Sugar rush leads where laughter flows,
Turning the mundane into grandiose.
Fruit chews mix with whispers of fun,
Curiosity's journey has just begun.

For in each bite, new wonders share,
Exploring the world, without a care.
Grab that candy, let's take a chance,
For curiosity makes the heart dance!

Art of the Snack Break

In between the daily grind,
A snack is what we seek to find.
Chips and salsa, oh what a dream,
We laugh and munch, our faces beam.

The clock ticks slow, the hunger grows,
So here we are, in munching prose.
Candy bars and cookies too,
A feast awaits, it's all for you.

With popcorn fluff and nacho cheese,
The snacking art is sure to please.
Each bite a chuckle, sweet delight,
We snack through day, and into night.

So grab a plate, and take a chance,
With snacks in hand, let's have a dance.
For on this trip, we truly thrive,
It's joy in bites that keeps us alive.

Cherries on the Path

A journey starts with little treats,
The cherry pit beneath our seats.
With licorice ropes in hand we roam,
Each tasty stop feels just like home.

We stumble, trip, but never frown,
With gummy bears, we'll never drown.
Peanut butter on the way,
Each mouthful turns our gray to play.

On a glorious trail of candy bliss,
We find the things that we won't miss.
Sour straws and lemon drops,
In every snag, a giggle pops.

So take a trip, and pack a snack,
On this wild route, there's no lack.
With bites of joy along the way,
We'll snack and laugh, come what may.

Culinary Curiosities

Strange delights on this buffet,
Who knew snacks could make your day?
Pickles wrapped in bacon tight,
A crunchy munch, oh what a sight!

With pretzels dipped in chocolate bliss,
Each bite's a giggle, you can't miss.
Savory cupcakes, tasted once,
A culinary ride, it's pure nonsense.

Explore the flavors, wild and bold,
In this snack world, we are consoled.
Taco-flavored ice cream delight,
A whirlwind treat that feels just right.

So dive into the taste unknown,
With every crunch, our laughter's grown.
For in this feast, we find our way,
Through curious bites, we laugh and play.

Cookies to Sustain the Spirit

Ode to cookies, round and sweet,
With chocolate chips, a perfect treat.
Baking magic fills the air,
Each bite a hug, we all can share.

Oatmeal raisin, snickerdoodle,
In cookie heaven, we are poodle.
Sprinkles dancing on the glaze,
Each nibble turns our frowns to praise.

So grab a cookie, take a seat,
Let laughter echo, feel the heat.
With each new recipe we make,
It's joy and crumbs that keep us awake.

Through chewy bites and frosted dreams,
We find our joy in cookie beams.
For when the times are feeling tough,
A cookie break is sweet enough.

www.ingramcontent.com/pod-product-compliance
Lightning Source LLC
Chambersburg PA
CBHW072214070526
44585CB00015B/1340